O HOLY NIGHT

How A New York Veterinarian and His Wife Saved Christmas

Dr. Richard Orzeck

Purrfect Love Publishing
Trumansburg, New York 14886

© 2015 by Richard Orzeck

Purrfect Love Publishing
PO Box 655
Trumansburg, New York 14886
(607) 387-3490

All rights reserved. Except for appropriate use in critical reviews or works of scholarship, the reproduction or use of this work in any form or by any electronic, mechanical, or other means now known or hereafter invented, including photocopying and recording, and in any information storage and retrieval system, is forbidden without written permission of the author.

Printed in the U.S.A.
Second Edition

ISBN-13:
978-1518687228

Cover illustration © by Annie Campbell

Dedicated to the memory of my
Father, who loved the journey of life on this
planet — this stunningly beautiful planet — more than
anyone I've ever met.
Richard C. Orzeck (1931 - 2006)

And
to every man, women, and child
who still have the courage to
believe in the miracle.

Preface

The following event, which took place on a snowy late December evening, is true. The account of the hundreds of dedicated medical and assistant volunteers—all anonymous—whose selfless behind-the-scenes efforts ensure the well-being and safety of Santa Claus and his reindeer on their annual journey around the world, is also true; likewise, the secret emergency medical centers described in the story really do exist. The details, however, of the actual locations of these emergency facilities, and the recruitment and training of the veterinary medical professionals and their personally handpicked assistants, have been modified sufficiently to protect the security and integrity of the mission.

I'm sharing this story with you, the gentle reader, with the full permission and encouragement of the Big Guy (Santa Claus) himself.

Dr. Richard V. Orzeck
Trumansburg, NY

CHAPTER 1 The Phone Call

It was just before five o'clock on Christmas Eve, 2005. I was nearly finished examining and treating what I had hoped was my last patient of the afternoon, when I heard the phone ring up the hallway in my private office.

It was the special phone.

The day's small animal office hours had been nonstop busy since my wife, Theresa, and I walked in the door earlier that morning. Really, really busy! Almost inhumanly busy! There had been an endless stream of coughing cats, vomiting dogs, and every other sickness imaginable, and we were both worn out. I remember thinking to myself in the middle of all that chaos that it seemed as if I was the only veterinarian in all of New York State who was seeing patients that day. It never stopped! Our sincerest hope before we had opened for business that morning was that it would be quiet and slow so that we might be able to close a few hours early in honor of the sacred holiday.

But it was not to be.

My first response to the completely unexpected phone call was a combination of surprise and disbelief. This was because, in all of the years since I had attended the special two-week-long, top-secret course shortly after my graduation from vet school, the plain and unassuming dark green telephone had just sat there quietly on the far corner of my physician's desk. Oh, I had used it over the years to call mission control in order to update the various status reports and schedule changes that were endlessly needed to help the organization accomplish its primary goal, but this was the first time the phone actually rang. And it rang while the annual mission was in progress.

With the realization swirling around and around in my mind as to what the phone call might ultimately mean for us, I found myself becoming a little bit uneasy, maybe even a little bit scared. I remember thinking to myself, *This can't be happening; maybe I'm just imagining the whole thing.*

But the phone just kept on ringing.

Not quite sure what I was going to do, I excused myself for a couple of minutes to the owner of the dog I'd been doctoring, walked out of the exam room and up the hallway to my office and, once in the room, still not knowing for sure if I was dreaming or not, just stood there looking at the phone. My wife had been out in the kennel feeding the hospitalized pets that were in the kennel room during the holiday when she, too, had heard the telephone ring.

She had stopped what she was doing, and she was now standing there beside me. Her presence brought me back to the reality of the situation. I looked at her, and she looked at me, and after a second or so of silence, she said, "Richard, you'd better answer it."

Still a little apprehensive about the whole situation, I paused for a few seconds longer. Then I silently nodded my head in agreement with her. I gritted my teeth, took a couple of deep breaths, and slowly picked up the receiver. Not knowing what else to say, I simply said, "Hello?"

It was the Big Guy on the other end of the line, and he was worried. Very worried! (The Big Guy was Santa's codename when he was airborne on his Christmas Eve journey.)

Our conversation was short, probably no more than a couple of minutes. He filled me in on what had happened and what his quick assessment of the injury was. I, in turn, with a professional calmness that surprises me even to this day, asked him several crucial questions. I wanted to know the extent of the injury, when it had happened, how he was treating it, how much pain the reindeer was in, and, most importantly, if the animal was well enough to stay airborne in order to make it to an emergency hospital if it would be necessary.

He answered my questions as best as he could. I then told him we'd head out to the planned rendezvous location and stand by just in case we were needed. And without taking the precious time to say good-bye, we hung up. Pausing for a second before speaking to Theresa, I looked out the window toward the clinic's parking lot and noticed that several inches of fresh, new snow had fallen upon it over the course of the afternoon, and that it was still coming down. I remember for a brief moment thinking to myself how beautiful — how stunningly beautiful — it all was. But the practical side of my nature didn't allow me to dawdle too long.

Turning back to Theresa, I quietly filled her in on what was going on. "Rudolph has been badly injured over Newfoundland. We're one of the emergency teams along the projected flight path, and it's very possible we may have to go out and take care of him. Santa wants us standing by. Just in case. We should leave as soon as possible."

I needed to say no more. Immediately she got back to work finishing her job of tending to the hospitalized patients, making sure they had plenty of food and water just in case we couldn't get back till morning. I went back to the exam room where I finished my examination and treatment of the patiently waiting sick dog.

When we both were done, we grabbed the special hidden bags of emergency reindeer medicine and supplies, took one more look at the animals in the ward room, closed down the hospital, turned the Open sign that hung on the front door around to the *Closed* side, and walked out into the peaceful, snowy, now-dark evening.

Before starting up our old four-wheel drive American Motors Eagle station wagon, I turned toward Theresa and said, "Well, I guess this is it; this is what we trained all these years for." A little worried about the whole situation, I quickly added, "Gosh, who in the world ever thought we'd be called upon to actually do it? I sure hope we can pull this off."

Theresa looked back at me and smiled her special reassuring smile. "Don't worry about it," she said. "You'll do just fine." Always the practical one, she then said, in no uncertain terms, that we should get going. And so we pulled out of our parking lot onto the dark highway and to our date with destiny. We were going to meet Santa Claus again. We were going out to do our best to help save a wounded, world-famous reindeer. We were, ultimately, perhaps even going to help save Christmas for the children of the whole of the Western Hemisphere.

Before heading out into the boonies, we stopped at our local grocery store and bought two boxes of peanut butter cookies and a quart of eggnog.

CHAPTER 2   Things Most People Don't know

There are a whole lot of things in this world that a whole lot of people have no idea exist, stuff that no sane, thinking person would ever, in a million years, give any thought to. This concept of not knowing was brought home to me profoundly once during a visit to, of all places on earth, Easter Island.

For those whose knowledge of world geography isn't too great, Easter Island is located in the middle of nowhere in the South Pacific Ocean halfway between Tahiti and South America. It is a tiny island about fifteen miles wide and twenty miles long and is one of the loneliest, most isolated places on earth. Its biggest claim to fame is its giant stone statues that mysteriously dot the island's landscape.

On our first visit to that astonishing place many years ago, after a five-hour journey from Tahiti across nothing but the cold dark blue Pacific Ocean, the pilot of our Boeing 737 had to first fly over the island before we could land, and then circle back around way out at sea in order to line the jet up with the eastern approach to the island's only airport.

As I looked out of the window down toward the ground, I was struck immediately by the enormous length of the island's single runway. It looked to be over fifteen thousand feet long, probably seven thousand feet more than our jet — or any other jet for that matter — would ever need. The next day while on a tour of the island, our guide told us that the runway was built courtesy of the United States government's National Aeronautics and Space Administration, NASA, as a potential emergency landing strip for the Space Shuttle.

This concept of providing for emergency assistance in case something went wrong with the Space Shuttle was something I'd never given any thought to. I would later learn that such specially designed runways exist all over the world: Honolulu in the central Pacific Ocean, in the Azores in the middle of the Atlantic Ocean, on the tiny island of Diego Garcia in the middle of the Indian Ocean, etc. Although in most cases, the airports serve primarily commercial or military needs, from the time of the Space Shuttle's launch until it is safely back within the bosom of mother earth, these airports' primary mission is to be ready in case something goes wrong.

I'm told the same preparations for an emergency occur on a more precise scale when the president of the United States has to travel. Preparations are made at every airport that Air Force One has to travel over on its way to the president's destination. Hospital and emergency care facilities, as well as all military and civilian defense centers near where the president is visiting, are all likewise kept on high alert. Even though none of the preparations—at least so far—has ever had to be used, the people are trained and the facilities they operate are in place.

Just in case.

And so it is—believe it or not—with Santa Claus and his nine faithful reindeer as they proceed on their yearly Christmas Eve around-the-world journey.

CHAPTER 3 A Trip To The Boonies

  As we started out on our forty-five-minute trip to the emergency rendezvous point, I filled Theresa in on what few details the Big Guy had given me over the phone. He told me that he'd just finished delivering his packages to the children in the Iceland/Greenland sector and was ascending to his regular transatlantic cruising altitude, when unexpectedly, a commercial passenger jet appeared from out of nowhere into the flight path of his reindeer and sleigh.

  He told me that he had no idea what this plane was doing in his vicinity. It had no business being where it was; his undercover air traffic controller at the airport in Gander, Newfoundland, had assured him just before he headed westward out over the Atlantic that he and his reindeer had the whole sky to themselves. (Later investigation of the incident revealed that the reason the airliner was where it was not supposed to be was that it had unexpectedly taken off thirty minutes late from JFK airport in New York City. It turned out that the pilot had apparently eaten some bad sugarplums at a Chinatown sidewalk market before his flight began and had a wicked case of diarrhea and couldn't get himself out of the toilet.)

Santa said the whole thing would have been an absolute disaster if it wasn't for the eternally alert eye of his lead reindeer, Rudolph, and Rudolph's immediate evasive maneuver of a hard turn of the sleigh to the starboard. Santa said that in the first few seconds after the near miss all had seemed fine, and it had looked as if they all managed to completely escape disaster. But then he noticed that, ever so slightly, they were for some unknown reason beginning to lose altitude.

Investigating the unexplained descent further, he looked ahead at his lead reindeer, and he saw to his great horror that Rudolph's lower left front leg was bleeding and that he was holding it up in what appeared to be an extreme amount of pain. Santa said he wasn't quite sure how it happened, but he thinks that as Rudolph was in the process of making the hard right turn that had saved everyone, the brave reindeer had placed himself in the path of the huge tailfin of the 747 jumbo jet. As the massive aircraft rushed on by, the very top of its tail slammed him in the leg.

From this point on, Santa still wasn't sure of the actual extent of his lead reindeer's injury. All he could say was that Rudolph was holding his left front leg up, there was blood staining the fur just below his knee, and that the courageous reindeer was doing his noble best to keep flying.

The Big Guy ended the phone conversation by saying that he was going to call in to work all of the emergency veterinary teams in the Canadian Maritime Provinces and, just to be safe, the Maine, New Hampshire, and New York (Theresa and me) regions of the Northeast United States sector. He specifically wanted us to stand by at the secret location known as Judd-Alpha.

After filling Theresa in on all that Santa had told me, we were both quiet for a long time. I'm not sure what her precise thoughts were, but I could imagine that in her mind she was already making preparations for any X-rays that would be needed, any surgical instruments, bandaging, or cast-making materials that she'd need to have ready for me to use. There were any numbers of one thousand other things that as my nurse/assistant she'd need to be ready to do, from calming down a very likely worried Santa to providing an emergency ration of feed and hay to the other restless reindeer.

I, surprisingly, didn't give much thought to the whole situation or to the medical responses and therapies I was possibly going to have to soon perform. And I guess that was because I'd trained and had done practice drills for years on all aspects of reindeer medicine and surgery. I felt confident — as long as Rudolph's injury wasn't too bad — that I could handle just about anything that could come up.

What I did think about was how thankful I was that the location the Big Guy decided upon as best for that evening's possible emergency would be Judd-Alpha. This meant that it wasn't going to be that long of a drive for us in the snowstorm to the secret hospital's location. The wind was beginning to really pick up and it was blowing the snow into big drifts, and it was unlikely the snowplows would come out on a Christmas Eve until the worst part of the storm had passed. I shuddered for a second when I thought about having to drive to the other two emergency centers we'd also been assigned to cover that evening, which were over one hundred and two hundred miles away, respectively.

We spoke, once again, just as we approached Judd-Alpha. Looking over at Theresa, I said, "Well, I guess this is it. I truly hope everything is going to be all right with old Rudolph. It sure does sound like he's in rough shape."

Theresa looked back at me, and I could see in the dim light of the car's interior that she was smiling that reassuring smile she has. "Don't worry, Richard, you'll do just fine."

Following the established protocol, I stopped alongside of the highway next to a long country lane that served as the driveway for the secret emergency hospital. Before turning and driving the car up into it, I made sure to look both straight ahead up the road and back behind us. As expected, being Christmas Eve and all, there was not another car to be seen.

I then turned left into the driveway and drove up behind the "abandoned" dairy barn. I knew that in a couple of minutes the blowing snow would hide any evidence of our being there. I then got out of the car, slid open the barn doors, got back into the car, and drove in. Once inside, Theresa walked back over, closed and locked the doors, and then rejoined me in the car.

Now all we could do was to sit there patiently and listen to the secure, worldwide radio transmitter to find out how Rudolph's emergency was playing itself out and to wait for the cell phone call we hoped would never come. From the constant chatter taking place between my colleagues on the ground close to Santa's location, it was beginning to sound pretty bad for the poor old reindeer.

CHAPTER 4 The Master

How we ended up in a lonely old cow barn out in the middle of the boonies on that cold and snowy Christmas Eve was something I'd never, in a million years, ever have thought possible. And as much as I'd like to believe otherwise, I know now that it wasn't by accident that we were now sitting there anxiously waiting for the emergency situation to unfold. I had been selected and personally groomed for this task from the very beginning of my veterinary education.

When I look back on it, I realize it all started after my first semester of vet school. Little did I know that two other members of my class and I had fallen under the watchful eye of "the master." The master, whose real name must (of course) be kept secret, operates at the veterinary college I attended, under the guise of a humble professor of bovine (cow) medicine. He's one of only three such persons in the whole world ever entrusted with this task.

No one knows for sure how long the ancient professor had been at the university. An endlessly royal pain-in-the-butt to generations of uppity college deans and a bane to the privileged existence of lowly vet students as well, if you asked anyone on campus about him, they'll tell you he'd been around forever.

There's even a rumor (spoken only in hushed and reverent whispers) that it was highly possible that he received his education in the medical arts from the great Hippocrates himself.

How long the great teacher has been around, however, doesn't really matter. Even though his job as a professor of bovine medicine has been a very fortunate side effect for the lives of all cows in this world, in actuality, it's all been just a huge, elaborate cover story; the master's primary task in life, since time immemorial, has been to discover and to recruit eligible veterinarians to be emergency reindeer doctors for what is called by insiders "the big ride."

Criteria for being asked to volunteer to provide emergency care to Santa's reindeer during the big ride are fairly strict and quite complicated. Potential team members must have caught the eye of the master during his bovine medicine lectures and hands-on barnyard laboratory sessions. It didn't matter how brilliant a student you happened to be with regards to passing examinations; it had more to do with his or her (yes, in spite of rumors to the contrary, women veterinarians are equally represented on the worldwide roster of volunteers) abilities to work with and not be afraid of large animals. A farming background was a plus but wasn't always necessary.

The two hardest criteria to meet, however, had nearly nothing to do with a future veterinarian's medical skills. He or she must also have been able to confide in, and provide a reliable, preferably lifetime partner, to assist wherever or whenever duty called. Also, the veterinarians and their assistant partners would have to be available and on call for nearly every Christmas Eve during the course of their lives. (In actuality, the teams are automatically granted one out of five holidays off; surprisingly, most teams decline the offer of time off, such is their dedication to the mission.)

Anyway, I'm not sure exactly what it was about me that caused the master to pick me out of my class of eighty-one other gifted students, but he did. Over the course of the rest of my freshman year, he'd either stop me in the hallways or outright invite me (and the other two candidates as well . . . but not at the same time) into the sanctified interior of his private office. Although normally noted for his abrasive, Attila the Hun teaching style (rumor has it he acquired the personality trait from the old Mongol himself), when he worked with the potential recruits for the Christmas Eve mission, he was always quite pleasant.

Once the time finally came for him to ask me if I'd be interested in joining the worldwide team, he probably knew more about me (and my wife as well) than I knew about myself.

CHAPTER 5   All Is Not What It Seems

People who drive around the highways and byways all over the world probably never pay any attention to the infinite number of what appear to be abandoned buildings and sheds that dot the countryside and cities. In some areas, they look like abandoned old cow or hay barns. In other areas, they look like unused tobacco drying barns, old fleabag motels, or rice storage sheds. In the big cities, they take on the appearance of old auto repair garages or vacated, bankrupt factory buildings. On the rare event that these places are ever noticed, you can almost bet that no one ever could have guessed these buildings' covert purpose.

Little could anyone ever know that many of these "abandoned" structures are really completely self-contained veterinary hospitals whose whole purpose of existence is to be available in case of an emergency with one of Santa's reindeer during their Christmas Eve ride. (It should be mentioned at this time that similar facilities involving emergency care for the Big Guy himself are also in place and are manned by my human doctor counterparts.)

Engineers and architects, who are also volunteers, search the planet to discover — or if necessary, actually build — suitable locations for these reindeer hospitals. They purchase the properties and then meticulously design each one to be a freestanding medical facility. When finished, they do everything in their power to hide the purpose of the building's capabilities. Each unit has its own electrical generators, its own X-ray unit, a state-of-the-art operating room, and enough emergency food supplies to feed a hospitalized reindeer for a month.

The security of the mission is always paramount in the designers' minds, and any violations of this security are rare. Exactly how such breaches are handled is a mystery. Rumor has it that there is an entire fleet of "vacant" Airstream travel trailers sitting around in retirement mobile home parks all over the place whose only function is to travel to a breached site, dismantle the hospital unit, or in the case of an extreme violation, completely destroy any evidence of a unit's mission.

Once, a few years ago, one of my fellow volunteers at one of the continuing education reindeer medicine conferences we have to attend asked the Big Guy about what happens during a breach. The student was firmly told that he should just pay attention to his job of saving the reindeer and not worry about anything else. It all had to do, Santa said, with the need to maintain plausible denial.

CHAPTER 6
Hurry Up! And Wait

As we sat there in our darkened car, we listened to Santa's progress on the transmitter. The latest word was that the bleeding on Rudolph's lower leg appeared to have stopped, and he was making a valiant effort to stay in the air. Consultations between Santa and the Canadian Maritime units had taken place nearly nonstop since the collision with the jet, and it had been agreed by all involved to keep the mission going as long as Rudolph was able to continue.

What would be done—if anything—with his injury depended on how much pain he was suffering. Even though he still held his leg up, the sleigh's flying altitude had somewhat stabilized. This gave the doctors and Santa some hope that all would be well. The decision was made to try to deliver the presents to the children of the Newfoundland, Canadian Maritimes, and Northeast United States sectors and see how well it would go.

It didn't go well.

While Santa was making his deliveries, Rudolph's lower leg began to swell. My Canadian colleagues all agreed that serious inflammation was setting in, and even though the reindeer might be putting on a brave appearance, he had to be hurting really badly. Within the next hour, his ability to maintain altitude became harder and harder. Finally, as they all were passing over the Vermont/New Hampshire region, Santa heard his lead reindeer let out a slight groan of pain. That was all he needed to make a decision.

    Right then and there, he decided to bring Rudolph in for a professional evaluation. He loved his reindeer as much as he loved all the children in the world. He would do anything — maybe even cancel Christmas? — before he would see any of these precious animals suffer. After further consultation, it was decided to bring him to Emergency Station Judd-Alpha, Theresa's and my location.

    Without a word, as soon as we got the news, Theresa and I got out of the car and began to get everything ready. I unlocked the secret control panel hidden behind a pile of hay bales and started up the electrical generator. After waiting the required couple of minutes for the engine to warm up, I turned on the lights and the heaters. Temporarily blinded by their sudden brightness, I waited a couple more seconds before doing anything else. While I was doing all this, Theresa began to clear away the hay that hid the entrance to the X-ray room and surgery suite.

    After regaining my sight, I walked over to the back

entrance of the barn and opened the door just wide enough for me to step outside. I then closed the big door behind me and walked a hundred or so feet out into the snow-covered hayfield. I needed to do two things: First off, I had to see if the barn, in spite of its interior being illuminated by the brightest lights known to man, was still dark and invisible to anyone passing by down on the highway.

Secondly, I needed a moment to myself to prepare, to psych myself up, and to take the whole experience all in. I took several deep breaths to try to relax myself. The air smelled clean and cool and fresh, and I could feel myself becoming reinvigorated. I remember tilting my head backwards and feeling the falling, wind-driven snow melting on my face. It was wonderful.

I was ready to go. After taking another minute in order to say a couple of prayers, I walked back to the barn. I started my car and backed it into the empty corner especially set aside by the engineers for that purpose. As her training had so well taught her, Theresa already had the X-ray machine turned on and warmed up, had the X-ray film cassettes loaded with film, had all the bandaging and casting material ready, and had the surgery room and any surgical instruments I might be needing laid out and set. My sincerest hope was that Rudolph wouldn't need any of this stuff. But if he did, we would be ready. Now all we could do was wait.

CHAPTER 7

The Brave Untold Story

There is a little-known event that occurred shortly after the time of our Lord Jesus' birth which, for unknown reasons, the authors John, Matthew, Luke, or Mark chose to leave out of their Gospels. The wondrous biblical story of the shepherds out tending their flocks around Bethlehem and their seeing a star in the sky announcing the birth of the newborn king is well-known to all; likewise is the tender nativity story of the infant Jesus lying in a manger surrounded and being warmed by the breaths of cows and sheep and donkeys.

But what was not told in the Gospels was that there were also reindeer at the nativity of Jesus. It turns out that one of the three wise men from the east was actually more from the northwest, from the area of the present-day countries of Russia and Finland. It was this wise man who brought along his herd of nine reindeer. And it's the exploits of these reindeer's selfless courage that is one of the greatest untold stories of all time.

It turns out that while the nativity scene we are all familiar with was playing itself out, a savage and bloody battle of monumental consequence was occurring in the pasture land surrounding the stable. King Herod in Jerusalem, upon hearing of a newborn king being born in Bethlehem, sent an armed patrol of Temple guards out to find the baby Jesus and then to kill him. But as the soldiers approached the stable, the reindeer, whose super-strong sense of smell detected the danger several minutes in advance, stood prepared to defend the infant Jesus, even if it meant losing their lives in the process.

And fight, they did!

Even though the soldiers had the advantage of having sharp, hardened-steel swords, the reindeer had for themselves just as good a battle weapon: their large antlers. After an hour of heated combat in which one after another of Herod's soldiers fell from their wounds or fled out of horror at the fighting skills of the fearless warrior reindeer, it was finally all over. The evil King Herod had lost, and baby Jesus would live to adulthood to carry out his earthly mission to save mankind.

But there was one very serious problem: The bravest warrior reindeer of them all, Rudolph, was mortally wounded. In the heat of the battle, one of the soldiers' swords hit its mark on the fearless reindeer and had seriously sliced off the end of his nose and muzzle. He now lay on the cold and rocky ground, profusely bleeding to death. Because there was nothing else they could do, his brother and sister reindeer comrades, either by instinct or divine guidance, all at once gently slid their huge antlers under the nearly lifeless body of their fallen comrade and carried him into the warmth of the stable.

Not quite sure what was going on, Mary, the mother of Jesus, was at first a little apprehensive about letting these huge animals too close to her newborn son. But her heart was softened when the word began to filter in of the brave defense they had just put up to protect them all, and she agreed to let them set the wounded reindeer down in the warm straw next to her son. As
Rudolph lay there clinging to life, struggling with every ounce of energy in his body to breathe through his severed mouth and nose, the baby Jesus began stirring in his cradle with an obvious great agitation. Seconds later, as if he could actually see and understand what was wrong with Rudolph, the infant reached out his right hand toward the reindeer.

Maybe it was the bright red blood-soaked head that caught His attention, perhaps it was the loud and heart-wrenching gurgling noise being made by Rudolph as he lay there gasping for breath; or maybe it was His infinite compassion at the sight of one of His Father's creatures suffering so badly that made him want to reach out and touch the wound. Whatever the reason was, seeing that Jesus wanted to be closer to this brave reindeer, the wise man from the north knelt down beside Rudolph and very gently lifted the reindeer's head upward so it would be in reach of the newborn king.

When the reindeer was close enough for him to do so, baby Jesus reached out his hand—just as he would in later life do with the lepers and the blind and all of the afflicted of mankind—and placed it upon Rudolph's bloody mutilated nose, and then he just left it there. All who watched on that cold winter's night were in awe of the miracle they were to witness.

As His precious hand rested upon Rudolph, the reindeer's nose began to glow with the radiance of a hundred suns. And as the minutes passed, the reindeer began to breathe normally; soon the animal was beginning to stir. After what seemed an eternity, baby Jesus removed his hand. In another minute, Rudolph—still very shaky—began to stand up. After yet another minute, with all his senses fully back in his control, Rudolph managed to reduce the intensity of his bright, shining, and now-healed red nose to near normal so it wouldn't blind everyone present. He then turned toward the baby Jesus and lowered his head in solemn reverence and thanks to the newborn king of Kings.

Baby Jesus looked back at him and smiled.

And it was from that holy night over two thousand years ago that Rudolph and all of the brave reindeer who fought so valiantly to save the infant Jesus were entrusted with the duty of helping all the children in the world on every Christmas Eve.

CHAPTER 8
Back To School

The lesson on how Rudolph and all of the other reindeer first obtained their special powers was one of hundreds of reindeer facts that Theresa and I learned at reindeer medicine and surgery school.

Upon my graduation from veterinary college, and after passing my state medical board exams, Theresa and I took two weeks' "vacation" to travel to Iceland. It was there that we told all of our family and friends we were going in order to relax, see the glaciers, and to perhaps do some birdwatching. The whole trip, as well as the birdwatching cover story, was arranged for us by the master himself.

After arriving in Iceland, we (and my other volunteer colleagues as well) were picked up by a private speedboat from a pier in the capital city of Reykjavik and then whisked away to an unknown island in the North Atlantic located just above the Arctic Circle. It was there that we all met our soon-to-be emergency reindeer medicine counterparts that had been recruited from all over the world.

The classes were divided into two groups: All of the veterinarians were in one group, and all of the support assistants were in the other. The assistants were taught all about handling and feeding the reindeer. They were shown how to set up and operate the emergency hospitals we veterinarians would all be working in. They learned how to run the X-ray machines, were taught important bandaging techniques, and to do everything else that would be needed in order to assist the veterinarians with any medical or surgical situation that might someday come up. Because he felt these most basic of skills were so important, Santa himself taught the classes.

We veterinarians were instructed on the finer points of reindeer anatomy, physiology, medicine, and surgery by the master and his two other counterparts (both of whom were equally ancient, with the same Attila the Hun personalities). Because all of us students had just recently graduated from a vet school somewhere, a lot of what the professors told us during the first few sessions was a boring review.

Reindeer (scientific name *Rangifer tarandus*), we were reminded, are members of the deer family and are related to wild caribou. They have been domesticated in Europe and Asia for about seven thousand years. They (and their cousins, the caribou) are the only members of the deer family where both the males and females grow antlers. Like cows, sheep, and goats, they eat grass and chew a cud. They've also developed a special ability to eat and digest the lichen (sometimes called reindeer moss) that grows on the surfaces of rocks in the Arctic. The reindeers' hair is extremely dense, which allows them to lie down or sleep on snow without melting it and getting wet. Again, all of this information was familiar to us.

What we students ***did*** find fascinating, however, were the classes in which we were taught about all of the theories regarding the special features that make Santa's reindeer so unique in the animal kingdom: their ability not only to fly, but to fly fast enough to circle the world in one night while pulling the enormous weight of a sleigh full of Santa and toys. I use the word *theories* here because there is no one easy or complete explanation of how the reindeer manage to get it all done.

If one were to give the matter any thought, what Santa and his reindeer accomplish every Christmas Eve is really quite mind-boggling. Figuring (very conservatively) that Santa must visit a little over one hundred million households in his twenty-four-hour trip around the world, this means that he has to make approximately one thousand one hundred stops per second. He and the reindeer, therefore, must travel nearly seven hundred miles per second (which is three thousand five hundred times the speed of sound)!

And not only must they go this fast, they must pull the sleigh containing Santa and the toys. If you calculate that there are two good children per each of the one hundred plus million households that celebrate Christmas throughout the world, this means the reindeer must pull (figuring a mere three pounds per child) six hundred million pounds; that's three hundred thousand tons!

How Santa and his reindeer are able to carry out such a gargantuan task was the source of much lecturing and discussion. The first thing pointed out to us by the professors was that we had to keep in mind what Santa and his reindeer do every Christmas Eve does indeed violate every law of physics known to man. Just the sonic booms from a flying sleigh traveling at three thousand five hundred times the speed of sound would shatter every window and Christmas tree ornament in the world!

Commonly told children's tales about the reindeer being sprinkled with fairy dust or eating magic corn were dismissed right off by our professors as being too simplistic. Likewise disregarded as being merely brainless babble were the really bizarre theories of the reindeer being supercharged by their use of steroids or by the selective eating of yellow snow that had been peed on by human shamans intoxicated on hallucinogenic mushrooms.

A theory whereby Santa's reindeer somehow manage to inflate themselves like hot air balloons was talked about at some length. Commonly referred to as "the gasbag hypothesis," the idea does a fairly good job of explaining how the animals could possibly obtain vertical liftoff. It doesn't, however, provide an explanation for how they're able to achieve forward motion once they're airborne. When asked jokingly by one of my classmates if this forward motion could result from the reindeer producing flatulence (farting), the master, who was not at all amused, looked my colleague sternly in the eye and asked, "Doctor, when was the last time you saw a picture of Santa wearing a gas mask?"

A similar hypothesis that suggests the reindeer possibly grow wings for one night a year was also brought up. Referred to as the "Pegasus phenomenon," the winged reindeer accounts nicely for how the animals might fly, but the theory falls short on many other levels. Just like any fixed-wing airplane or jet, reindeer with wings would need a runway to take off from in order to generate lift. This would be OK in the rural areas of Santa's delivery zones, but would not at all do in the cities. Also, in order to be able to support the weight of a five hundred pound animal, the wingspan would have to be thirty-two feet across, which would make flight impossible in an urban environment. Most importantly, the theory doesn't address the sleigh full of toys. Because of its massive weight, without some method of generating lift for itself, all the sleigh and Santa would do is hang limply behind the flying reindeer as they flew.

The most complicated theory put forth in an attempt to understand all of the Christmas Eve marvels — and the least understood by us mortal students — was what the teachers referred to as the "Einstein paradigm." Or, put more simply, it was a hoped-for theory of everything. This mind-boggling hypothesis took us on a mental journey into the realm of the quantum mechanics that we students had all struggled so hard with in our pre-med, undergraduate college days; it was some pretty heavy-duty stuff.

After making sure once again we students understood that everything they were about to tell us was just speculation, the professors proceeded to speak at great length about how the reindeer might be using a not-yet-discovered ability to create alterations in Einstein's so-called space/time continuum. This distortion in the fabric of time could be the driving principle behind what allows the reindeer to be in a thousand places at any instant of time. Put more simply, by their as-of-yet-unknown ability to control time, the reindeer are able to make use of a form of quantum teleportation. This would give them the capacity to be in an infinite number of places at any one time. (I told you this was heavy stuff!!!)

As the ancient and learned professors spoke on and on and on, I remember looking around the classroom and seeing the glassed-over eyes on all of the faces of my fellow student colleagues and feeling a bit of relief. This stuff about cosmic worm holes, fractal vortex shedding devices (the reindeer antlers), string theories, and nine-dimension universes was going completely over all of our heads. Not a bit of it was getting through to us.

And, as the lectures went on and on, it all got a little hard to listen to. After all, we were doctors, not astrophysicists. Finally, fearing the endless theorizing would never end, one brave (very brave) student raised her hand and spoke up: "Please, sir," she said, pointing to the master, "what do you personally think gives these reindeer their ability to do this seemingly impossible task every Christmas Eve, and how can we as mere veterinarians do anything to help?" An uneasy hush followed as we all waited for his reply.

After what seemed like an eternity, the master stood up. He looked slowly and silently at each of us anxious students, the wisdom of thousands of years blazing in his eyes. He'd heard this question before, and he was, therefore, not offended. When he finally spoke, it was with the humbleness of a saint. "Doctors," he said, "I, myself, personally asked that very question of both Sir Isaac Newton and of Albert Einstein. Both of those great scholars gave me the same answer: 'Know the mind of God, my humble pilgrim, and then you'll understand.'" After the master spoke, all were silent.

A couple of moments passed. Apparently not completely convinced that the master had properly answered her question, the student persisted. She asked, "Sir, that's all well and good, but my question was, what do *you* think?" Another reverent hush once again filled the classroom.

With the grace and dignity of a person who has lived a long and thoughtful life, he looked directly at her, smiled, and respectfully answered her question. (He'd heard this one before also.) "My dearest Doctor and colleague," he said, "I believe that what the reindeer do is a miracle; a miracle of everlasting love, just like the miracle that took place in a little manger on that cold, Holy night over two thousand years ago." And he said no more.

CHAPTER 9
Rudolph Arrives

People are always asking me when they visit my veterinary practice with their pet, "Doc, why is it that you and your wife are always going on vacations?"

I usually smile when asked this innocent question and always answer something like, "I need to get away to relax, have a few beers, and lie on the beach and work on my golden tan," or, "We need to satisfy our various wanderlusts, to see new things, meet new people, etc."

I resist the occasional temptation to tell people that sometimes they drive me crazy, and if I don't get away, I'll go bonkers, and they'd have to remove me from my office in a straitjacket.

What I don't tell my treasured clients is, of course, that we have to go away sometimes in order to attend reindeer medicine and surgery continuing education conferences every few years. Santa, being a North Poler, tends to favor cooler locations for these meetings: Iceland, Finland, Patagonia, etc., although, every once in a while, he'll throw in a Saint Martin or Hawaii location.

It is at these conferences that we emergency vets update our knowledge and skills of everything reindeer. Sometimes I've been bored to tears with all of the repetition, repetition, and still more repetition of medical and surgical procedures I'd already heard of a hundred times. But in that lonely old barn on that freezing cold night, as we waited for the Big Guy to arrive, I was thankful to God that I paid attention.

And as we sat there waiting, another call finally came through on the radio from Santa. He said that he was just about two minutes away, and to go ahead and open the hospital door. By the time I got it unlatched and the snow cleared away in order to push it open, Rudolph and his brothers and sister reindeer were standing there waiting to come in. That was just the way we were told they do it. There were no bells, no noise, no warning of any kind: They were just there!

Right off the bat as I approached the animals, I could tell something was terribly wrong: Rudolph's nose, instead of being a blinding, glorious light, was now a muted and dull shade of yellow. My first thought was that the fearless and loving reindeer must be hurting really, really badly. Grabbing hold of his harness, I looked down toward the snow-covered ground and saw that the shin of his left front leg was a swollen glob of fur and snow and blood.

And no sooner had I made this quick assessment than I saw Santa trudging through the snow toward me. Pulling off his glove, he reached out and shook my hand. The distress and concern in his voice was obvious. "Good to see you again, Doctor. Thank you so very much for coming out tonight. I pray we didn't wait too long with Rudolph."

"Sir, it's my honor to help," I said.

He then walked around the front of the reindeer over toward Theresa, who was already at work starting to remove Rudolph's harness in order to disconnect him from the sleigh. "It's lovely to see you, too, my dear lady," he said. "Thank you also for coming out on this cold, cold night."

Seeing that he was nearly in tears with worry about his beloved reindeer, Theresa stopped for a precious second what she was doing, walked over, and gave Santa a big hug. "Good to see you again, too, Santa; I wouldn't miss this for the world." Stepping back slightly so she could look him in the eye, she added, "Don't worry, sir, Rudolph will be just fine. My husband has trained for years for this night, and he's ready to do whatever it takes. Now, let's get this harness off and get the old boy inside."

CHAPTER 10 A Bloody Mess

After disconnecting Rudolph from the other reindeer and sleigh, we grabbed him by his bridle, and then Santa and I walked him into the barn/hospital. Before closing the door, Santa turned around and said to his other loyal reindeer, "Dasher and Dancer and Prancer and Vixen; Comet and Cupid and Donner and Blitzen, please wait out here for just awhile. We have to try to help Rudolph." One by one, because they truly understood what Santa just said, they all nodded their heads. Then we closed the door behind us. Theresa would join us as soon as she gave the waiting reindeer something to eat.

Once inside the barn, in the warmth and good lighting, while Santa held Rudolph by the bridle, I began to examine him. As I've already said, his nose was very pale; this bothered me a lot. When I opened his mouth and looked at his gums, instead of being a nice, bright pink color, I saw they were also very pale. This observation, as well as the fact that his heart rate was twice as high as it should be, told me that he'd lost a tremendous amount of blood and would soon be in shock. This meant that I would, therefore, need to stabilize Rudolph with a blood transfusion and intravenous fluid therapy before I could seriously address his injured leg.

(Even though Santa's reindeer are "immortal," they are still prone to mortal problems. Their bodies function just like those of all reindeer: they need to eat, they need both exercise and rest, they must defecate, and, most importantly, they do feel pain. And even though we veterinarians have no exact idea of how these reindeer accomplish their miraculous Christmas Eve journey, we do know that they need to be in peak physical and mental condition to pull it all off. This was why Rudolph was unable to maintain his altitude or speed. He pain was so severe, that even with his strong will and determined mind, his body was just too weak to go on.)

By this time Theresa had joined us, and as if she was reading my mind, she began shaving the hair on Rudolph's neck over his jugular vein. She knew I was going to have to give him a transfusion of whole blood. As Santa held the reindeer's bridle, I scrubbed the shaved region with antiseptic, inserted an intravenous catheter into the vein, attached the bag of life-giving blood to the catheter, and opened up the valve to start the transfusion.

Once I was sure the transfusion was working properly, I looked up at Santa and saw he was wobbling and a little bit shaky; I'm not sure he was too crazy about seeing all of that blood. Theresa, who apparently saw the same thing I did, said, "Santa, why don't you go over around the corner to the sitting area and rest for awhile. I have for you there your favorite peanut butter cookies and a quart of fresh eggnog." (There was a pint of his favorite brandy there as well.) "The doctor and I will take it from here."

Obviously relieved at no longer having to watch, he let go of the bridle. He stepped back a few paces, looked his reindeer in the eye, and said, "Now, Rudolph, my dear, dear friend, let the doctor and his wife take care of you. I'll be right over there." He pointed to the little lounge area the hospital engineers had designed especially for this purpose. But before he sat down, he walked over to the door to the outside, opened it up, and stepped out. Although we couldn't hear all of what he was saying, we knew he was trying to reassure Rudolph's fellow reindeer that their leader would be all right.

Not wanting to waste any more time, Theresa and I got back to work. With the warm, life-giving blood now flowing into Rudolph's veins, the gash on his leg could be addressed. As Theresa focused the portable surgical light on the leg, I knelt down for my first good look at the wound. All I could see was a frozen mass of hair, blood, snow, and open flesh. I remember thinking at the time how awful it looked. I asked Theresa to bring me a bucket of warm water.

When she'd done so, I grabbed a handful of gauze pads, dunked them into the warm water, and began to carefully clean the area around the wound. I was especially cautious when I got close to the gaping wound itself; I didn't want it to start bleeding again. After removing the majority of the ice and hair and blood, I could see that the airliner's tail fin had created a deep nine-inch-long laceration that ran obliquely up and down the reindeer's leg between his ankle and knee. Examining the wound very carefully, I discovered the injury had penetrated all the way down to the bone and tendons, but I couldn't tell for sure by looking if any were broken or damaged.

Standing up, I bent down with my left hand, grabbed Rudolph's lower leg, and gently picked the foot up a couple of inches. He resisted at first, letting out a little snort of pain, but after a couple of seconds, he allowed me to continue. With my right hand below the hoof to keep it from moving, I tried to flex and extend the lower leg. I needed to see whether or not the bone was completely broken and also if there were any severed tendons. After flexing and extending the joint several times, I was fairly sure there were no major breaks in the bone. But just to be safe, we decided to do X-rays.

As Theresa set up the portable X-ray machine, I reassessed Rudolph's cardiovascular system. With the first bag of blood nearly empty, he was starting to look a little better. His gums were now a little pinker and his pulse was stronger, all of which meant his blood pressure was stabilizing. Also, the light emanating from his nose was beginning to brighten.

I also felt a little better myself, knowing he was improving. After doing a quick test to find out his exact red blood cell count, I decided he wouldn't need any more blood to be transfused. When the bag he now had attached ran out, I would change it over to just a simple saline drip. This would help maintain his blood pressure in case anything went wrong during his surgery.

When the X-ray was set up, I shot two films, one view from the side and one view front to back. This allowed me to analyze any possible fracture to the bone in three dimensions. When Theresa returned from the developing room, she put the films on the X-ray viewer. When I saw them, I'm sure a big smile came to my face; there were no breaks in any of the leg joints or bones. Things were starting to look up for old Rudolph.

While Theresa took down and put away the X-ray machine, I went over and filled Santa in on the situation. First off I told him there were no broken bones. (I could tell by the look on his haggard face that he was very pleased by the news.) I then sat down in the chair next to him and told him what I thought we should do. I nibbled on a peanut butter cookie as I spoke.

CHAPTER 11   The Good News

I told him that even though there were no broken bones, there was a lot of damage done to the muscles and other tissues around the wound. There was also possible damage to one or two of the extensor tendons of the foot, but I wouldn't know this for sure until I got Rudolph into surgery. But I quickly reassured him that as bad as all I just told him sounded, there didn't appear to be any damage done to any of the major blood vessels or nerves of the leg. With just some minor surgery and a little bit of supportive nursing care, he should recover just fine.

What I had to say next, however, made me just a little bit nervous. I had made a medical judgment regarding Rudolph's condition and would now have to stick my neck out and hope to God that I was correct. "Santa," I said as calmly as I could, "barring any other significant findings I might make during his surgery, it is my professional opinion that, with the help of the blood transfusion he's been given, and with the additional support of the intravenous fluids he is now receiving, I see no reason why you and Rudolph can't continue your journey after we are finished suturing up his leg."

There was a minute of silence as Santa considered my decision. As I watched him and waited for his response, he gave me not a single indication as to what he was thinking. And I was sort of glad he took the time to think over what I'd told him. He would be the one (or so I thought at the time) who would ultimately have to decide to continue or to abort this year's Christmas Eve mission. "What about his pain?" was Santa's first question.

Knowing Santa, and knowing how much he truly loved his reindeer, I was ready for his question. "Santa," I said, "I plan to do the surgery after doing a local nerve block to control the pain of any cutting or stitching I'm going to have to perform. It's my professional opinion that this pain control will last about three to four hours after the surgery is finished.

"Since you already have the Pacific Islands, Australia, Asia, Africa, Europe, the Canadian Maritimes, and a little bit of the Northeast United States finished, that leaves you only the rest of North and South America and the Pacific Islands on this side of the International Dateline to deliver to. In short, you probably have only another seven to eight hours to go before you're back to home base." As we sat there, a strange thing seemed to be happening with the lighting in the barn: It was getting just a bit brighter.

I gave Santa a couple of seconds to think about what I just said before continuing. "I can guarantee you, sir, that the wound is going to start hurting when the local anesthetic wears off. But even though there is a lot of bruising and other tissue damage in and around the wound, the pain shouldn't be too severe. But if or when it seems to become too much for him to bear, you can do one of two things: You can give Rudolph a few tablets of an excellent oral painkiller that I'll send you out with, or" — and I said this second part carefully so as not to upset Santa — "you can let the reindeer just tough it out until you get home."

There was silence as Santa reflectively stroked his great white beard. As we sat there, I noticed again that the whole room was getting brighter and brighter. My first thought was that something was going wrong with the electrical generator.

Santa then asked, "What about his wound? Will it be OK in the bad weather as he's flying? What about when we get back home?"

All the while he spoke, even though I was giving him my undivided attention, I couldn't take my mind off of the room. The lights just kept getting brighter and brighter.

I never got the chance to fully answer his question.

Concerned that there was a problem with a possible electrical surge, I was about ready to excuse myself for a second from our conversation in order to walk out into the generator room, when suddenly, Theresa hollered for me to get out into the examination area. And she meant right now!

Without a second of hesitation, I jumped up and ran around the corner to where she and Rudolph were standing. Santa was directly on my heels. As I entered the room I could see that she was having a very hard time holding old Rudolph down. I also discovered the source of the brightening light: It was his shining nose.

Santa ran over and grabbed his reindeer by the bridle. "Whoa, whoa," he calmly said to Rudolph. "What's the matter, old boy?" After a couple of seconds of Santa's gentle touch, Rudolph's light dimmed somewhat, and he settled back down. The two of them spent a few minutes in what appeared to me to be a silent conversation. When it seemed like they were finished, he turned toward Theresa and me and spoke.

"Doctor," he said, "Rudolph wants to continue. He's been listening to our conversation about him and was afraid I would not want to continue the mission tonight because of his potential pain. So he let us know his feelings on the matter in the only way he could, by shining his light to tell us he was fine. He **wants** to go on and finish taking care of all the remaining children in the world. He loves them all so much. He doesn't care if it hurts him or not: He **has** to finish his important mission."

"All right," I said. And that was that.

CHAPTER 12 The Surgery

Theresa and Santa then moved the brave reindeer into the surgery room and held him as I gave him the local nerve block; I did this so he wouldn't feel any pain as I stitched his wounded leg. He twitched around a little bit at me as I inserted the needle full of lidocaine in several locations all around the margins of the wound, but he was an ideal patient otherwise. When the numbing was complete, I clipped any excess hair from around the cut and then scrubbed and sterilized the area. Before beginning to sew the wound shut, I once again analyzed the damage.

Two of the muscles had been completely sliced in half, and another one was only partially cut. Much to my delight, however, was the fact that all the tendons looked in good shape. And so, after scrubbing my hands and gloving up, and with Theresa assisting me, I began the process of suturing everything inside the wound that was torn or ripped apart. It took about thirty-five minutes to sew everything back together. When I had finished, I closed the skin hole with eighteen nylon stitches.

I wiped the leg with a towel to dry it off as well as I could and applied a sterile bandage over the wound. Over this I placed several wrappings of waterproof tape to try to keep the surgery site protected from the harsh weather. I removed the catheter from his neck and finished the job by giving Rudolph a shot of long-acting penicillin in his butt muscles. His little jump when I gave the injection told me once again he wasn't too crazy about needles.

I then grabbed hold of the reindeer's bridle from Santa and Theresa and personally walked him back out into the waiting area; I wanted to see and feel and get a good sense — for my own peace of mind — of whether Rudolph was doing OK and would be able to finish his evening's work. He walked with barely a limp. He seemed remarkably well.

I then patted him on his muzzle and said, "All right, old buddy, it's up to you now. Please take it as easy as you can; it's going to hurt you a little bit when the lidocaine wears off, but I think you can handle it."

After I finished speaking, the reindeer looked at me with an expression that I can't put exactly into words.

I don't know if it was my imagination or not, but as I gazed into his big, beautiful brown eyes, I thought I heard him tell me, "Doc, I'll be all right. Don't you worry a single bit." He then backed up slightly, raised his mouth up to my face, and gave me a big, juicy lick on my right cheek. I knew for sure at that instant that everything would be fine.

The magic of our moment, however, didn't last too long. Santa and Theresa had walked over to where we stood, grabbed hold of his bridle, and started walking Rudolph toward the door. The mission had to go on. As they walked away, I just stood there for a few moments.

My job was done.

CHAPTER 13 The Brave Reindeer Returns

When they opened the door, the blast of cold winter air blowing into the barn brought me back into the reality of the situation, and I walked outside to join them. As the two of them worked to hook Rudolph back up to his fellow reindeer and the sleigh, I briefed Santa one last time on the animal's aftercare. I told him to be sure to constantly monitor Rudolph's altitude during flight. This would be the best way to tell if he was in pain or not. I told him that when he got back to the North Pole, the master himself would probably assume charge of Rudolph's recovery. I then said good-bye.

As busy and in a hurry as he was, Santa stopped for a second what he was doing. He stood straight up, walked toward me, wrapped his massive arms around me, and gave me a big hug. Patting me hard on my back, he said, "Dr. Richard, I can't thank you or your wife enough for all you've both done. The children of the world thank you also." He then backed up and helped Theresa finish harnessing the animals.

When they were done, he gave Theresa a big hug, and they both spoke something I couldn't hear. Tears began to roll down both their cheeks as Santa started to walk toward his sleigh.

As he climbed into the sleigh and sat down, he waved at us one last time. An instant later he yelled, "On Dasher and Dancer and Prancer and Vixen; on Comet and Cupid and Donner and Blitzen; onward Rudolph, show us the way, my precious old friend." Then there was a bright flash of light, and they were gone. And Theresa and I were left standing alone in the cool and now lightly falling snow. We savored the moment, and I wished it could last forever.

CHAPTER 14 O Holy Night

But Theresa, who, thankfully, could always be depended upon to be practical, broke the spell and said, "Richard, we need to get on the radio and alert all of the other emergency centers of what we've done here tonight. It's procedure."

"All right," I grudgingly said, and we walked back inside the hospital and closed the door behind us.

I spent the next twenty minutes or so speaking with my colleagues at all of the veterinary emergency centers in the rest of the Western Hemisphere—as well as those in the rest of the world who were still awake and following all that was happening—explaining to everyone what I'd just done, and what my possible concerns were for the remainder of the mission.

Theresa started cleaning up. She only had to do a quick job and clean up any obvious blood and debris; in a couple of days, people passing by on the lonely country road would notice a beat-up old Airstream trailer with a flat tire parked outside the barn. If they paid any attention to it at all, they would probably just assume the owner had left it there and had gone for another tire. Little would they suspect that a professional cleanup crew was inside the run-down old dairy barn, restocking and completely scrubbing from top to bottom the place where a miraculous old reindeer was kept alive just a couple of nights before.

By the time we both finished all of what we needed to do, word was starting to come in over the radio that Santa was finished with his Central and South American deliveries and was over the Rocky Mountains. Rudolph was doing fantastic!

As we shut down the generator and backed our car outside, the first thing we both noticed was that it had stopped snowing. We both got out of the car and walked over to close the barn door. After locking it and making sure it was secure, we just stood there, taking all of the experience in. The stars now shone in a clear, cool, night sky. It was awesome.

I looked at my watch. The luminous dial told me it was quarter past midnight. Turning toward Theresa, I said, "Merry Christmas, my dear love." Grabbing my hand and squeezing it tightly, she looked me in the eye and said, "Merry Christmas, my dear husband."

Pulling her toward me, I reached over and kissed her.

It was a merry Christmas.

Made in the
USA
Columbia, SC